Team Players

Story by Diana Noonan
Illustrations by Alisha Monnin

Contents

Chapter 1

Wide Awake

It was Friday night and Carter was feeling anxious. The rain had been torrential all day, and it was still pelting down outside. If it didn't stop soon, the sports ground would be a swamp.

Carter picked up Mum's phone from the kitchen table and called his friend Joel.

"I know, I know," said Joel when he heard Carter's voice. "If it doesn't stop raining soon, they'll cancel our game. Or we'll have to turn into a swim club."

Carter tried to laugh, but he didn't feel like joking around. The fact was, there was something else that was playing on his mind. It was something he didn't want to confront because he knew it would make him feel miserable as *well* as anxious.

"Catch you later – hopefully tomorrow," he told Joel as he ended the call and put down the phone.

Carter went into the living room to say goodnight to Mum and then headed to bed. But almost an hour later, he was still wide awake. He reached for the small flashlight he kept under his pillow, switched it on and shone the light over his bedroom walls. They were covered in rugby posters – each one a gift from Dad, who always looked out for them whenever they were for sale in shops. Carter flicked the beam of the flashlight from one poster to another, lingering on any that featured one of the Green Ferns.

The Green Ferns was his favourite rugby team, and the current Green Ferns captain, Dan Shellbrook, was the best player of them all. Dan was a legend, and before long, he would be a world megastar – Carter was sure. He'd played twelve tests and he was the youngest captain the Green Ferns had ever had. Just as importantly, he was a good sport – he never lost his temper and he always played fair.

Carter let out a long sigh. He was passionate about rugby (that was the word Mum used). He loved playing it, being a spectator, following it on TV – sometimes he even dreamed about rugby!

Saturday morning rugby was the thing Carter most looked forward to all week, and now the rain meant his game would probably be flooded out.

There was a soft knock.

"Wondering if rugby will be cancelled?" Mum asked from his bedroom doorway.

Carter looked up.

"I saw the light from your flashlight flickering about," she said.

"Why does it always have to rain on Friday night?" asked Carter, miserably. "If I was a Green Fern, I'd never have to worry about my game being cancelled."

"If you were a Green Fern," said Mum, "you'd be playing under a covered stadium if the rain was this heavy."

Carter trained his flashlight onto a book about the Green Ferns captain, Dan Shellbrook, which was propped up on top of his desk. Dad had sent it to him just last week.

"I still can't believe Dad actually got to talk to Dan while he was waiting for him to autograph the book!" said Carter. "If I ever got the chance to talk to Dan Shellbrook, I think I'd lose my voice!"

Carter sank back down in his bed and stared up at the ceiling.

"Is the rain *all* that's worrying you?" asked Mum, after a minute or two. "Or is something else bothering you, Carter?"

Carter opened his mouth to say something, then hesitated and closed it again. He wanted to confide in Mum, but the problem was so complicated, he didn't know where to begin. Carter was also concerned that if he did manage to explain the situation to Mum, she might then go to Mr Martin, his rugby coach, about it. Players always found out when a parent had been to see Mr Martin, and they often gave their teammates a hard time about it.

"I'm okay," said Carter, at last, but Mum didn't look convinced.

"Well, whatever it is," she said, smiling, "we've got a reason to feel more optimistic about your game being on tomorrow."

"Why?" asked Carter, gloomily.

"Because the rain has stopped," she replied. "Listen!"

Carter lay very still. "It *has* stopped!" he said.

"I'd say it's game on, tomorrow," said Mum, as she took Carter's flashlight from him and switched it off.

Carter pulled the covers of his bed up to his chin.

"Do you think I have a chance of being a Green Fern one day, Mum?" he asked.

"If you work hard enough," replied Mum, as she went out the door. "I think anything's possible. But only if you get some sleep!"

Chapter 2

Carter's Concern

Carter did get to sleep eventually, but not before he'd done a lot of thinking about Dylan James.

Dylan was the same age as Carter, twelve, and Carter had known him since they were both six years old playing Ripper Rugby together. Now, Dylan was the only other player in the Under 13s who had the same potential as Carter.

Dylan and Carter didn't see a lot of each other because they went to different schools, but they always said hi if they met down the street. Mostly, Dylan was what Carter thought of as "a rugby mate". The two of them had fun together whenever they helped out with fundraising for the junior rugby club. When they played rugby in another town, they always shared a seat on the bus on the way, and Saturday mornings in the club room after their game, they always raced each other to wolf down their cookies.

What Carter appreciated most about Dylan was that he was a good sportsperson. Even though the two of them were always competing to be player of the day, Dylan didn't let that interfere with how he behaved on the field. He always played fair – or, at least, he always *used* to play fair. And that was the problem.

Carter rolled over in bed and wished he could concentrate on getting to sleep. But he couldn't get Dylan out of his mind. There were just a few weeks of junior rugby left to play before the season was over for the year, and after that, Carter and Dylan would start playing for the senior rugby club. At senior level, players were put into grades for the first time, which was why the senior club coaches were now coming along to the Saturday morning junior games. They were watching out for the most promising players – the boys who would get to go into the Under 14s A-Grade team next season.

Carter really wanted to make it into the Under 14s A-Grade team, but to impress the senior club coaches, you needed to demonstrate your skill on the field. And to do that, you had to create as many opportunities to get the ball as possible.

Getting the ball wasn't too difficult for good players like Carter and Dylan, but, for some reason, Dylan had decided to go one step further. It was as if he was trying to attract the coaches' attention by proving he was a better player than Carter.

Last Saturday, he and Carter had been on the same side. But Dylan had made sure he always got to the ball first, even when Carter was closer to it. There was something else Dylan was doing, too – and it was more than not fair. It was as if he was trying to make Carter lose his nerve whenever he was around Dylan.

In the middle of the scrum, where no one could see, Dylan had scraped Carter's shin with his boot. It had really hurt, and Carter was certain Dylan had meant to do it. In the same game, when Carter had run in to catch a high ball and Dylan had been really close, he'd called out, "You're going to miss it, Carter!"

Carter was starting to suspect that Dylan wanted more than to be picked for the Under 14s A-Grade team – he wanted to be chosen to captain the team!

Whatever Dylan was up to, he wasn't playing fair any more, and Carter didn't know what to do about it. Carter definitely wanted to get noticed by the senior coaches, because everyone said that being in the Under 14s A-Grade team could be the start of a rugby career. But if Dylan kept pushing him around on the field, Carter would end up looking like a loser.

Before Carter went to sleep, he decided he'd give Dylan one more chance to be a good sportsperson, like before. But at tomorrow's game, if Dylan was still picking on him and playing rough, Carter would have to do something about it.

Chapter 3

Up and At 'Em

When Carter woke the next morning, the sun was shining and the rain really had disappeared. He felt so much better after his sleep, he even started to wonder if he was imagining the stuff about Dylan. Maybe last Saturday had just been a one-off thing.

Outside, Carter heard a car pull up. It would be his Uncle Len dropping off his cousin Nikky before he went to work. Nikky was a netball player, but Mum always gave her a ride to the courts, and when she wasn't playing at the same time as Carter, she liked to come to his matches and cheer him on.

"Up and at 'em!" said Nikky a moment later, standing at the door to Carter's bedroom. "Get your gear on and pack your bag! Your mum says we're leaving in twenty minutes."

"Sure thing!" said Carter, leaping out of bed and laughing as he saluted.

"And don't forget to eat your breakfast!" called Mum. "Those Under 14s coaches will be watching again, today, and you'll need some energy if you're going to impress them!"

Suddenly, Carter didn't feel so positive. He did want to impress the coaches. He just hoped there was some way he and Dylan could both show off their skills and still be rugby mates on the field.

When Mum drove into the sports ground car park, the first people Carter spotted were Dylan and his dad, Mike. They were standing beside their car looking at Mike's phone.

"Morning, Lisa!" Mike called out to Mum. "Morning, Carter! We're just looking at today's draw. You and Dylan are on field three, Carter. You're playing against each other as the Reds and the Blues."

Carter felt himself relax a little. At least if he and Dylan were on opposite sides, they were *supposed* to be competing against each other.

"You're both on the wing," Mike told Carter. "It's going to be an interesting game, isn't it!"

"Why did he give you that weird smile?" Nikky asked Carter, as Mum went to the club room to deliver some cookies she'd made.

Carter shrugged, but he'd seen Mike's strange expression, too, and it made him feel uncomfortable. It was as if he knew something Carter didn't.

Nikky went to find Mum, and Carter waited for Dylan to walk over to field three with him. When he didn't come along, Carter went on his own and caught up with Joel, who was also heading there.

"I thought the fields would be flooded this morning," said Joel when he spotted Carter. "I thought we'd all be wearing life jackets!"

Joel began chuckling at his own joke, but Carter wasn't in the mood for laughing. He glanced back over his shoulder to see if Dylan was following, and what he saw had him worried. Mike had his hands on Dylan's shoulders. Their heads were almost touching, and it looked as if Mike was whispering advice.

Out on the field, Carter helped himself to a blue jersey from a basket and pulled it over his head. Dylan arrived shortly afterwards and put on a red one. Standing close by, where they could hear anything that was being said, were two coaches from the senior club. They were listening intently.

"Over here, boys!" called Mr Martin, signalling for the players to come into a huddle. "We've got a wet field out here today, so what do we need to concentrate on?"

Carter saw Dylan's hand shoot up.

"More spilled ball," said Dylan.

"That's right," said Mr Martin. "Which means, what?"

"We have to focus on handling the ball on the ground," replied Dylan, glancing over at the senior coaches to make sure they were still listening.

It's starting already, thought Carter. *Dylan is trying to show off before the game has even begun.*

"Anything else?" asked Mr Martin.

Carter put up his hand before Dylan could.

"We have to grip the ball hard as soon as we fall on it," he said in a loud voice.

"You're onto it, boys," said Mr Martin. "Now, on the field, everyone. And remember, good sportsmanship makes for a great game!"

As Carter jogged onto the field, he saw Mum and Nikky arriving on the sidelines, and Mike bringing up the rear. Mum and Mike were the loudest supporters, and they usually stood side by side. But today, Mike was making his way further up the field from Mum.

"Good luck!" said Carter, taking up position beside Dylan.

Dylan kicked the heel of his boot into the soft ground and didn't reply. Somehow, Carter wasn't surprised.

Chapter 4

Bad Play

The game kicked off. Side by side, Dylan and Carter jogged up and down the field, but play was concentrated at the Blues' end. Suddenly, the ball broke free. As soon as Carter could see it was coming his way, he manoeuvred into position so he was ready to take the pass he knew was coming his way. Dylan had realised what was happening, too, and began jostling with Carter. Carter sidestepped his way free, ready to catch the ball, but from the sidelines, he heard Mike shouting.

"Step up to the mark, Dylan!" he called. "Don't give him a chance!"

Distracted by Mike's comment, Carter watched the mud-covered ball slide through his fingers, and as he bent to retrieve it, Dylan's boot smashed down onto his hand. Carter rolled onto the ground in pain as Dylan kicked the ball into touch.

"All right, lad?" asked the referee, running over to Carter as he blew his whistle.

"I'm fine," said Carter, getting up off the ground. He was determined not to let Dylan know just how much his hand hurt.

"I *saw* that!" Carter heard Nikky call from the sidelines. "Bad play!"

"What happened?" asked the ref.

"Nothing," said Carter. "I just tripped and bent my wrist back."

He knew it wasn't true, but if the ref suspected there was bad feeling between him and Dylan, he'd be watching them both like a hawk.

For the remainder of the first half, Carter and Dylan shadowed each other, but there was no chance for Dylan to play rough without being spotted, and the score remained nil–all. But the second half was a different story, and it wasn't just Dylan who was being unsporting. On the sidelines, Mike's comments grew more and more negative.

As Carter ran towards the ball, he heard Mike shout, "You're offside, Carter!" Carter knew he wasn't, but Mike's comment was enough to make him glance over at his teammate. And by the time he'd done that, Dylan had the ball.

Carter wished Mum had heard what Mike had said, but he was standing too far away from her. And suddenly, Carter realised Mike must have planned it.

At the end of the game, the score was 5–3 to Dylan's team. From the sidelines, Carter saw Mike give Dylan a thumbs up. Nikky saw it, too. Carter could see her watching them. She looked furious!

On the field, the Blue and Red teams assembled in a line, ready to shake hands with each other as they filed off the field. When it came time for Dylan and Carter to shake, Carter held out his bruised hand. Dylan wouldn't look Carter in the eyes, but he said, "Good game," loudly enough for the senior coaches to hear him.

"Good game!" said Carter back, just as loudly.

After the players had changed out of their rugby gear, everyone went to the club room for their hot drink and cookies. Dylan stayed well away from Carter.

"That doesn't look good," said Mum, when she saw the red mark on Carter's hand. "I saw you go down in the first half. What happened?"

"I tripped when I was trying to pick up the ball," said Carter.

"No, you didn't!" said Nikky. "Dylan kicked you. I saw him do it."

Mum looked shocked, but before she could ask anything, Nikky said she had to go for her netball game.

"I'm getting picked up at the gate," she told Mum. "Catch you both later."

As she headed out the door, Mr Mahaka, the club president, tapped on his glass with a spoon.

"Attention, please, everyone! Attention!" he said. "First things first, we have our player of the day certificates to give out."

Carter was disappointed not to get the Under 13s certificate, but he was pleased that Dylan didn't receive it, either. Then, Mr Mahaka said he had a very exciting announcement to make.

"The club," he said with a grin, "has just been informed that the Green Ferns will be coming to town at the end of the month to play their first regional warm-up game."

The noise in the room was deafening as everyone started talking at once.

"Can we go to the match?" Carter asked Mum over the commotion. "Can we?"

"You bet," replied Mum. "I wouldn't let us miss it for the world!"

At the other end of the club room, Dylan and Mike looked just as pleased. Maybe, thought Carter, the excitement of the Green Ferns' visit would take Dylan's mind off playing rough. He sure hoped so.

Chapter 5

The Giveaway

On the way home from Saturday rugby, Mum and Carter dropped by the supermarket to pick up Gran's groceries. When they arrived at Gran's to deliver them, they discovered Nikky's mum, Aunty Kate, was visiting. They all decided to have takeaway at Gran's for dinner that night once Nikky got back from her game, so Mum and Carter didn't get home until late. That meant it wasn't until mid-morning the next day that they went online to buy tickets for the Green Ferns game.

At first, when they logged in and couldn't find any tickets, Mum thought there must be something wrong with the booking site. But after a while, when they still couldn't find any, she was really puzzled.

"I can call Joel," suggested Carter. "He told me that he and his parents were going to get tickets."

"Good idea," said Mum, passing Carter her phone. "See what you can find out."

When Joel answered, Carter didn't even have time to ask about the tickets before Joel came out with the whole story.

"What do you mean 'all the tickets have sold out'?" asked Carter, trying not to shout.

"*Already*?" asked Mum, listening intently. "But we only heard about the game yesterday afternoon." She sat down hard on her chair.

"It must be a mistake," said Carter into the phone, but Joel was quite sure it wasn't.

"Mum says everyone she's spoken to from the rugby club has had the same problem. She was talking to Dylan's dad, and he told her it's because the warm-up games are being played in smaller centres this year. He said all the city clubs are bulk buying the tickets as soon as they go on sale."

"Did Mike and Dylan get tickets?" asked Carter, suddenly.

"No," said Joel. "They had the same problem."

"The game's being played on *our* sports ground, and we can't even watch it!" moaned Carter.

"Mum says it'll be on TV," said Joel, "but it won't be the same."

"It's not fair!" said Carter.

And when he explained to Mum what Joel had told him, Mum felt exactly the same way!

It soon became clear that the rugby club committee didn't think it was fair, either. At least, that's how Mum put it when she came looking for Carter at lunchtime and found him making a sandwich in the kitchen.

"Listen to this!" she said. "I've just had a text from the club. It sounds like Mr Mahaka complained to the Green Ferns' managers about our club families not being able to get tickets."

"Good on him!" replied Carter.

"And now," continued Mum, "it seems a few tickets *have* been found."

"How many is a few?" asked Carter.

"Just a dozen," said Mum.

"But how will the club decide who gets them?"

"Mr Mahaka has it all sorted," said Mum. "They'll go to next Saturday's players of the day."

Carter did some sums in his head. "That's only six tickets," he said. "Who gets the other six?"

"Each player of the day will get to take one adult with them," said Mum. "That sounds fair, doesn't it?"

"I guess so," said Carter, but he was worried. If Dylan was already targeting Carter just to get noticed by the senior coaches, what would he be like if he was playing for a ticket to a Green Ferns game?

"Oh, wait!" said Mum, looking back at her phone. "I missed something. It's at the end of the message. Now this is exciting, Carter!"

"What is it?" asked Carter.

"The Green Ferns have also invited one young player to carry the ball onto the field at the start of the game and place it ready for kick-off."

"How are they going to choose someone for *that* job?" asked Carter.

Mum scrolled down on her phone.

"Mr Mahaka has decided it will go to next Saturday's Under 13s player of the day – a sort of farewell award because the Under 13s will be moving on to senior rugby next season."

"So, the Under 13s player of the day will get to see the match *and* carry the ball onto the field?" asked Carter. "That person could be me, Mum!"

"It could be," said Mum. "But it could also go to someone else, so don't get your hopes up too high. The main thing is to play your best next Saturday. That's all you can do."

Carter took a bite of his sandwich. He was going to have to think about next Saturday's game very carefully, because one thing was sure – Dylan would be doing everything he could to be the Under 13s player of the day!

Chapter 6

T-shirt Tussle

Carter couldn't get next Saturday's game out of his mind. He *had* to win player of the day. At school on Monday, his teacher asked him if he was okay because he didn't seem to be concentrating in class. But that was nothing compared to what happened later in the week.

The trouble began on Wednesday night, when the senior coaches turned up unexpectedly to watch rugby practice – something they hadn't done before.

"They really *are* looking for next year's A-Graders," Carter heard someone say. "They make me nervous."

Carter left his gear bag on the bench of the changing room and went to the bathroom. When he came back, he put on his shorts and jersey, but he couldn't find his boots anywhere.

"Has anyone seen my boots?" he asked, looking around for them.

Dylan was heading out the door in a big group of boys, and outside, Mr Martin was blowing his whistle. If Carter didn't find his boots soon, he wouldn't be able to practise.

"There's a pair in here," said Luke, a player from Carter's class at school. He was looking into a shower cubicle.

"Thanks," said Carter, as he grabbed his boots from the shower and tugged them on. Thankfully, they weren't wet. He ran outside and onto the field. Dylan looked up at him, furtively, and Carter was in no doubt about who was responsible for hiding the boots.

Dylan was on his best behaviour during practice, and Carter knew why. Without the distraction of a game in progress, the coaches could clearly see what everyone was doing. But if Carter thought he was safe from Dylan until Saturday, he was wrong.

Carter's birthday was a few weeks away, but Dad had sent him some early birthday money because he knew there were Green Ferns t-shirts for sale in the shops. It was all to do with promoting the game that was coming to town.

"I'm going to get the shirt with Dan Shellbrook on the front!" Carter told Mum as they headed to Duncan's, the sports shop in the mall.

Inside Duncan's, Carter tried on a Dan Shellbrook t-shirt. It was a little bit big, so he and Mum left it at the counter while they went to look for a smaller size. When they couldn't find any more Dan shirts on the rack, they returned to the counter to get the one they'd left there, but someone was already buying it! It was Dylan, and Mike was with him.

"Oh, sorry," said Mum, "that one's ours. We just left it at the counter for a minute while we went to look for another size."

"I've just paid for it," said Mike.

"I'm terribly sorry," said Mrs Duncan, turning red as she looked at Mike and Dylan. "I thought you must be the people who left it at the counter."

"No," said Carter. "That was us."

"Is there another Dan Shellbrook shirt out the back?" asked Mum. "There are no more on the rack."

"I'm afraid not," said Mrs Duncan. "They've been very popular this week, and we've sold out. We do have other Green Ferns t-shirts, though."

Mum looked at Mike, as if she was expecting him to give the t-shirt back, but he didn't. He just picked it up and went to walk away.

"Excuse *me*!" said Mum, becoming angry. "This isn't fair!"

Mike shrugged. "Sorry about that," he said, turning his back on her. "I can't help you."

"That is unacceptable!" said Mum, as Mike and Dylan walked out of the shop. "Come on, Carter, we'll try somewhere else for a Dan t-shirt."

In the end, Carter and Mum couldn't find another Dan t-shirt anywhere in town.

"Dad said he's going to buy one online for me," Carter told Mum later that night, after he'd spoken on the phone to Dad. "He's going to courier it to me."

"That's nice," said Mum.

"It's still not fair that Mike and Dylan took the last Dan shirt from the shop when it was ours," said Carter.

"It certainly isn't," said Mum. "I didn't think Mike was that sort of person. It just goes to show – you never know what people are really like until they want something you want."

Chapter 7

Winding Up

When Mum and Carter arrived at the sports ground on Saturday, Nikky was with them. Joel's father, who always made a huge batch of scones for Saturday morning rugby, came over to the car carrying them.

"I hear the Green Ferns have asked the club to cater the post-match function on the big day," he said to Mum, as she got her basket of cookies out of the back seat. "I might even get to see one of them having a cup of tea while I'm handing out my scones!"

"Here's hoping!" laughed Mum.

"I'll help serve the tea if I get to see one of the Green Ferns!" volunteered Nikky, with a laugh.

Carter noticed the rugby kids weren't saying very much at all. He wondered if they were feeling as nervous as he was about their games, wondering if they'd get chosen as player of the day and score a ticket to the match.

Mum found the Saturday draw on her phone. "You're in the Blues again, Dylan's in the Reds," she said, when Carter asked. "You're on field two. Take care out there. Everyone's going to be trying harder than usual to be player of the day."

The ref thought so, too. Before he blew his whistle for the Under 13s game, he gave everyone a stern talking-to about being sporting and playing fair. Carter hoped Dylan was listening. But as it turned out, Dylan was working on a new plan to be best on field – and it almost succeeded!

Dylan's bad behaviour started a quarter of the way through the first half, when the Blues' first five-eighths kicked the ball forward. Carter found himself running towards it, hoping to catch it on its second bounce and run with it. When he heard someone coming up behind him, he knew it would be Dylan. Dylan was a faster runner than Carter, so Carter expected Dylan to outrun him to the ball. If he did, it wouldn't matter, because Carter would go in for a tackle. But what happened next was plain unfair.

Just as Carter was reaching for the ball, Dylan pushed him from behind. It wasn't a big push – not like a shove that would be noticed by the ref. In fact, anyone on the sidelines would be unlikely to see it.

But it was enough to throw Carter off balance, and as he pitched forward onto the ground, Dylan landed on top of him. The ball bounced ahead and was picked up by another player from the Reds, who kicked it into touch.

Carter and Dylan scrambled up off the ground. Carter was so furious at Dylan, he felt like pushing him right back. But that wasn't going to help him win player of the day, so he quickly backed off. However, before he'd taken more than a step away, Dylan jumped back and put his hands up in front of his face. Carter suddenly realised what was happening. Dylan was trying to make it seem to anyone watching like Carter was going to hit him. It was a trick to get Carter in trouble. Carter quickly turned and ran towards a group of teammates before the ref wondered what was going on.

But the push was only the beginning. Later on, when Carter was running for the ball again, Dylan tackled him before he'd even got possession and Carter fell and went sliding along in the mud.

"Not fair!" he heard Nikky call out crossly.

"Early tackle!" shouted Mum from the sidelines. "Early tackle, ref!"

"He had the ball when I tackled him!" Dylan shouted back at her.

"No, he didn't!" said Nikky.

"Keep the game moving!" called Mike. "Come on, Carter, get off the ground. You're not hurt."

Carter looked around for the ref, but the game had moved on. The ref hadn't seen what Dylan had done. He was blowing his whistle and the coaches were clapping as the Reds scored their first try of the match.

At half-time, after Dylan had tried to upset Carter for a third time, Mum came over to where the players were having a drink of water.

"What's got into Dylan?" she asked, taking Carter aside. "I can see he's trying to wind you up."

"What's got into *Mike*?" asked Carter. "They've both got it in for me."

"I can see that!" said Mum.

In the second half of the game, Carter wanted to get back at Dylan, but it was too risky. He was afraid anything he did would be noticed by the ref or the senior coaches. So, Carter decided to keep his distance from Dylan, even if it meant letting him win the ball. At full time, when the Reds had won the game 14–5, Carter stomped angrily off the field.

"I haven't got a hope of getting player of the day," he told Mum and Nikky when they met him at the door to the changing room. "It will go to Dylan."

"I wouldn't be so sure of that," said Mum, kindly. "Your team didn't win, but you were both the two best players on the field. It could go either way."

"I thought you played really well," said Nikky. "Sorry I can't stay to hear the results, but I have to get to my netball game."

Carter went to get changed. At least they wouldn't have to wait long before they found out.

Chapter 8

Player of the Day

When Carter went into the club room for his hot drink and cookies, Dylan was already there – and he was wearing the Dan Shellbrook t-shirt.

"Did you see what Dylan's got on?" Carter asked Mum, when he found her in the kitchen piling cookies onto a plate.

Mum nodded, but before she could say anything, Mike walked into the kitchen with some cups and started putting them in the dishwasher. Usually, Mum and Mike would be laughing and joking with each other, but today, they didn't say a word.

Carter wished the whole competition thing between him and Dylan would just go away. Trying to impress the senior coaches was taking all the fun out of Saturday games. And as for trying to win player of the day and the Green Ferns tickets, it was enough to make him think about giving up rugby!

That afternoon in the club room, Mr Mahaka didn't have to ask everyone to quieten down. As soon as he stood up, there was a hush, and the room went silent. Mr Mahaka started by saying how sorry he was that almost everyone had missed out on tickets to the Green Ferns game. Then, he said that he hoped parents would use the match as a way to fundraise for the club.

"We've been asked by the Green Ferns' manager if we'll help with catering and traffic control on the day," he said. "The club will be paid for it, and anyone who helps will be invited to the post-match get-together in the club room. The Green Ferns will be there, so it will be a chance to meet them!"

There was a round of applause.

"In the meantime," said Mr Mahaka, "we do have our special tickets to give away to our players of the day, so let's get started."

Mr Mahaka began with the little kids and worked his way up to the Under 12s. As each lucky player came up to the front to collect their tickets, everyone clapped.

When it came to announcing player of the day for the Under 13s, Carter glanced over at Dylan. Mike had his hand on Dylan's shoulder. Dylan was smiling, as though expecting to hear his name.

But Mr Mahaka had a surprise in store for everyone.

"I'm afraid we haven't made our decision yet about the Under 13s player of the day," said Mr Mahaka. "There are a few things to consider, so we'll be sending out a text about it later in the week."

Dylan looked over at Carter. His smile had changed to a stormy expression.

"Well, what do you make of all that?" asked Mum, when she and Carter were getting in the car to go home.

Carter shrugged. "I might ask Joel if he wants to ride his bike to the pool with me this afternoon," he said. "I'm over rugby."

"You don't really mean that," said Mum.

But Carter wasn't so sure.

Carter and Joel spent the afternoon at the pool. As they zipped down the water slide and bodyboarded along the river ride, at last Carter relaxed and stopped going over and over the morning's game in his mind.

On the way home from the pool, he and Joel rode past the mall to look at the Green Ferns display they'd heard was in the window of Duncan's sports shop.

"Dan Shellbrook is awesome," said Carter, looking

through the glass at the full-sized cardboard cut-out of his rugby hero. "Did you see the way he lifted Phil Brady in the line-out when they played that last test against Australia?"

"He's got so much muscle," said Joel.

Suddenly, Carter heard his name being called from the other end of the mall. It was Dylan. He was with a couple of his friends.

"Let's go," said Carter to Joel. "I don't feel like talking to Dylan."

"That's right! Run away!" taunted Dylan, as Joel and Carter walked quickly out to the street and got on their bikes.

"What was that all about?" asked Joel, as he pedalled along beside Carter.

"Nothing," said Carter. "Just some stuff that happened at the game today."

But as he rode home from Joel's later that afternoon, Carter knew that things between him and Dylan were getting serious. Perhaps it really was time to call it a day with rugby.

Chapter 9

The "Perfect" Plan

Monday came and went without any word about the Under 13s player of the day. At school, rumours started circulating. Some of the rugby boys in Carter's class said they'd heard there wasn't going to be an Under 13s player of the day. They said Mr Mahaka had made a mistake about the number of tickets. Someone else said the Green Ferns were coming to town during the week to check out the field, and that Mr Mahaka had asked them to present the Under 13s tickets.

Carter tried to ignore the rumours. But now all he could think about was getting to see the Green Ferns play.

"Not knowing which Under 13s player is going to get tickets is very hard on everyone," said Mum that afternoon, when Carter arrived home from school.

Mum picked up her phone to check for messages and put it down again. "I don't know why Mr Mahaka is taking so long to decide."

By dinner that evening, Mum must have checked her phone at least a dozen times. But when news finally arrived, it wasn't by text.

"Who's that?" asked Carter, when there was a knock on the door after dinner.

Mum went to check.

"Mr Mahaka, come in!" Carter heard her say. "This *is* a surprise."

"Hello, Carter," said Mr Mahaka with a grin, coming into the kitchen.

"Hi," said Carter.

Mr Mahaka was holding an envelope. Carter's heart started beating loudly in his ears as he guessed what was inside.

"Congratulations," said Mr Mahaka, passing the envelope to Carter. "Here are two tickets to the Green Ferns game."

"Thank you!" said Carter.

"Goodness!" said Mum. "How exciting."

Carter opened the envelope and looked inside.

"I've never seen the Green Ferns play," he said. "Neither's Mum. But now we'll both get to go to a live game!"

"Does that mean you're taking me as your guest?" asked Mum with a grin.

"Of course I am!" said Carter.

Then, Carter remembered that he'd also be carrying the ball onto the field at the start of the game. He opened his mouth to ask about that, but Mr Mahaka beat him to it.

"The best news, Carter," continued Mr Mahaka, "is that you won't be alone when you run onto the field with the ball at the Green Ferns game."

Carter looked puzzled.

"The reason we delayed the Under 13s player of the day decision," said Mr Mahaka, "is that we have *two* very promising players in your age group. The coaches couldn't decide which of them should receive the tickets."

"So, what did you do?" asked Mum.

"We went back to the Green Ferns management to see if they could give us two more tickets. That way, we could have two Under 13s players of the day," said Mr Mahaka.

"And they said yes?" asked Mum.

"They did," said Mr Mahaka. "They always keep a few tickets in reserve."

"Who's the other lucky player?" asked Mum.

"Dylan," said Mr Mahaka. "And he's taking his dad!"

"So, Dylan and I will both be running onto the field with the ball?" asked Carter.

"Exactly!" said Mr Mahaka, beaming.

Carter's stomach tightened into a hard knot.

"Perfect," said Mum.

Carter could see she was forcing herself to smile.

"Well, I'll head off and let you two celebrate," said Mr Mahaka. "Meanwhile, please keep the exciting news to yourselves until I get back home and send out a text message to all the club members. Such a pity not everyone can see the game."

"It is," said Mum, as she opened the door for Mr Mahaka to leave.

"Thanks again for the tickets!" said Carter, trying to sound brighter than he felt.

When Mr Mahaka had gone, Mum looked at Carter.

"You and Dylan are going to have to sort out your differences before the match," she said.

"I know," replied Carter, "I'm just not sure how."

Chapter 10

A Big Mistake

Now that they both had tickets to the game, Carter hoped Dylan might not be so mean to him on the field. But he was wrong. In the lead-up to the Green Ferns game, Dylan was still out to impress the senior coaches. And he still thought the way to do it was to show them he was a better player than Carter.

"He tracks me wherever I am on the field," Carter told Nikky that night on the phone, when she called to ask him how the game had gone. "He's like a shadow. Why doesn't he pick on someone else?"

"Because the only way to prove he's a great player is to be better than the best," said Nikky. "And you are the best player in the Under 13s, Carter."

If Carter thought he'd had enough of Dylan's behaviour, Mum was at her wits' end with Mike's.

"He's such a bad example to other parents on the sidelines," she said, when Carter had finished talking to Nikky. "As well as only cheering for Dylan, now he's beginning to question the ref's decisions!"

"I know," said Carter. "We can hear him when we're on the field."

"And he's making some very loud and unpleasant comments about other players if they get in Dylan's way! It's not what a parent should do!"

Carter winced. Some of the stuff Mum had begun shouting at Saturday games wasn't so great, either. The sooner rugby season was over, the better. Then he'd start playing cricket. That was one game that Dylan *didn't* play.

Carter might have been feeling down about his own rugby games, but that didn't stop him from getting excited about the Green Ferns arriving in town. On the Friday before the match, he and Joel cycled downtown to the hotel where the team was supposed to be staying. A group of other kids, including Dylan, were already there outside the hotel doors.

If the Green Ferns were inside, they were well and truly out of sight. However, it wasn't long until one of the hotel staff came out with a pile of postcards of the team.

"Help yourselves to these," they said, smiling as they handed the postcards out to everyone.

Carter went up to collect one for himself and one to give to Nikky the next time he saw her, and found he was standing next to Dylan.

He decided he'd better say something to him, or it would be really awkward when they met at the Green Ferns match.

"Guess we'll get to meet some of the players tomorrow night …" he said, as Dylan took a postcard.

Dylan didn't answer.

"When we carry the ball onto the field," added Carter, looking for some kind of response.

"When *I* carry the ball onto the field," said Dylan, as he turned away.

Carter felt as if he'd been punched in the stomach. He wished he hadn't said anything to Dylan, but it was too late. And now he was dreading tomorrow night more than ever.

Carter knew he couldn't tell Mum what had happened outside the hotel. If he did, she might go to see Mike about it and that would just make things worse.

"Mr Mahaka came by," said Mum brightly when Carter got back home. She held up a sports bag. "He left this for you."

When Carter looked inside the bag, he found a brand new, crisp pair of snow-white rugby shorts and a new rugby shirt in the club colours.

"How about that!" said Mum. "When you run onto the field carrying the ball tomorrow night, you'll be representing the whole club. This will be something you remember your whole life, Carter."

It sure will, thought Carter. *But not in a good way.* Why hadn't someone realised that two people couldn't run onto a field with one ball? The club might have been trying to do the right thing by choosing two Under 13s players of the day, but they'd made a big mistake.

Chapter 11

Battle for the Ball

On the night of the Green Ferns game, Carter had to be at the club room a whole hour early.

"Mr Mahaka said it's to do with security," said Mum, as she drove him to the sports ground. "Once you go into the dressing room, you can't go out again until you and Dylan run onto the field."

Carter took a deep breath.

"Good luck," said Mum, as she dropped him off.

At the door to the club room, a security officer took Carter to the dressing room. Carter kept looking around for the Green Ferns, but he couldn't spot any of them. He supposed they were still at their hotel.

Inside the dressing room, Dylan was already there, putting on his shorts and jersey. Carter got his new gear out of his bag and put it on. Then, he and Dylan sat silently at either end of the dressing room.

The minutes ticked by. Finally, a man arrived carrying a net with three rugby balls in it.

"You must be Carter and Dylan," he said. "I'm Todd. I work for the Green Ferns." He smiled warmly at them. "Congratulations on being chosen as the ball boys for the match."

"Thanks," said Carter, as Dylan came to stand beside him.

"So," said Todd, taking two of the balls out of the bag, "these souvenir balls are for you. One each."

"They're signed!" said Dylan.

"By the team!" said Carter, turning the ball over in his hands. "That's awesome. Thank you!"

"And this is the match ball – the one you'll carry onto the field," said Todd, taking it out of the net.

"Thanks," said Dylan, taking it from Todd before Carter had a chance.

"Sorry, you will have to wait here for another forty-five minutes," said Todd. "Just before the game starts, I'll come back here for you and take you out to the field. After you've carried the ball out and placed it ready for kick-off, I'll take you to your seats, okay?"

"Okay," said Dylan, brightly.

"Okay," Carter said with a nod.

After Todd had gone, Dylan began slapping the match ball against the palms of his hands, as though he was warming it up.

Carter felt so angry, he thought he might explode! At the other end of the dressing room, a door whined open. Carter couldn't see who it was who'd come in because the doorway was hidden behind a row of lockers. The door banged shut again. Whoever it was must have gone back out.

Dylan kept slapping the ball from hand to hand until, finally, Carter just couldn't keep quiet any longer.

"What makes you think you're the one who gets to carry the ball onto the field?" he demanded. "We both got picked to do it."

"Well, there's only one ball," sneered Dylan, "and it looks like I'm the one who's got it."

"Todd gave it to both of us," said Carter.

"I'm carrying this ball onto the field," said Dylan. "You can tag along behind, baby. Or you can stay here in the dressing room. Suit yourself."

Carter stood up and walked over to where Dylan was sitting.

"You think you can do whatever you want!" he said. "I'm sick of you, and I'm sick of the way you've been playing on Saturdays."

"Don't know what you're talking about," said Dylan.

"How about last Saturday on the field, when you

pushed me?" asked Carter. "How about that illegal tackle? You can't even play fair. You're pathetic!"

Carter lunged forward and tried to snatch the ball from Dylan's hands, but Dylan refused to let it go.

"You can't get the ball from me!" he told Carter, angrily. "Just like you can't get it from me on the field. You're useless, Carter!"

"Boys! That's *enough*!"

Carter got such a fright, he actually jumped. Dylan almost dropped the ball, and when they both looked in the direction the voice had come from, Dan Shellbrook was standing at the other end of the dressing room glaring at them. He had his Green Ferns uniform on and he looked like a giant.

"I've got a game to play in forty minutes," he said. "I came in here for some quiet so I can focus before I go on the field. And all I can hear is you two arguing."

"Sorry," said Carter.

"Yeah, sorry," muttered Dylan.

Dan turned, as if he was going to go out of the dressing room, but then he stopped.

"You're Dylan and Carter, the ball boys for the match, right?"

Carter nodded. He couldn't believe Dan knew their names.

"Well," said Dan, coming towards them, "you'd better tell me what the problem is. You two have got an important job to do tonight, and you need to get it right."

Dan sat down on the bench opposite Dylan and Carter.

"C'mon," he said. "Out with it!" He pointed at Carter. "You first."

Chapter 12

Side by Side

Carter couldn't believe that Dan Shellbrook – the captain of the Green Ferns – was actually taking time to talk to him. And right before a match!

"I g-guess ... I guess ..." he stammered, "we both want to carry the ball onto the field," he told Dan.

"Is that all?" asked Dan. "Sounded to me like you two have been having problems for quite a while." He looked at Dylan. "Well? Am I right?"

Dylan went red, and even though he only told Dan half the story, Dan seemed to understand exactly what was going on. Especially about how both Dylan and Carter wanted to get into the Under 14s A-Grade team next year.

"Working your way to the top in rugby isn't easy," Dan told them. "But you're never going to get anywhere if you don't look out for each other."

Carter listened closely. He could see that Dylan was paying attention, too.

"Coaches aren't looking for heroes," said Dan. "They're looking for players who know how to be part of a team. *Team players*. They want to see how you can get the ball to another player. They want to know you'll pass when you can't run yourself."

Carter nodded, taking in the words.

"You might have both got player of the day this time," said Dan, "but as soon as you get higher up in the game, you're going to have to stop thinking of yourselves if you want a future in rugby."

Carter wanted to tell Dan that it wasn't his fault; that it was Dylan who had started the whole thing. But if he did, he'd only be thinking about himself – which was what Dan had just told them *not* to do.

"As for carrying this ball onto the field," said Dan, taking it from Dylan, "there's no 'I' in rugby. You're going to have to do this together, as a team."

"How can two people carry one ball?" asked Dylan.

"Top rugby players don't just use their bodies," said Dan. "They use their brains, as well. I think you two can come up with a plan to make it happen."

Dan looked up at the clock ticking on the far end of the dressing room. "But while you're figuring it out, do me a favour and keep your voices down, because I need some quiet time to focus."

Dan went back behind the lockers at the far end of the dressing room. Dylan and Carter began talking in low whispers.

By the time Todd came back for them, they knew exactly how they were going to take the ball onto the field. And planning it together had actually been fun!

"Ready?" asked Todd, as he led Carter and Dylan out to the edge of the field.

"Ready," said Carter and Dylan at the same time.

"Good luck!" called Todd, as Carter ran onto the field with the ball in his hands.

As Dylan came up behind him, Carter passed the ball back to him – carefully – so that he wouldn't miss catching it. Then it was Dylan's turn to run ahead and pass the ball back to Carter.

Back and forth went the ball between the two boys as the spectators began clapping. By the time Carter and Dylan had reached the centre of the field, the clapping had turned to waves of cheers. Then, as Dylan placed the ball carefully on the ground and stood back to study it, the crowd grew silent.

Just as everyone watching must have been wondering what was going to happen next, Carter took an exaggerated step towards Dylan and pretended to whisper something in his ear. Dylan nodded his head up and down, and patted Carter on the back as if he was thanking him. Then, he went up and adjusted the ball. Finally, Carter and Dylan gave each other a huge high five and ran off the field with their arms around each other's shoulders. The entire crowd of spectators stood up and began stomping and cheering in the stands.

"That was *amazing*!" said Todd, as he led Carter and Dylan back through the dressing room and outside to their seats. "We've never had ball boys do anything like that before. In fact, some of the Green Ferns said to me that they think you've stolen their show!"

Chapter 13

Win-Win

It wasn't until they were at the post-match function in the club room that Dylan and Carter saw each other again.

"Cool game!" said Dylan to Carter.

"That drop kick from Dan, right at the end!" replied Carter. "I mean, how did he get the ball over from that angle?"

"Thanks," said a voice behind them. "It wasn't easy, I can tell you!"

Carter spun around. Dan was towering over him – over everyone in the room!

"You two did a great job of getting that ball onto the field," he told Carter and Dylan. "I'm proud of you boys. I hear your parents are here tonight, too. How about I meet them?"

Carter went to find Mum, and Dylan caught Mike's eye across the room and waved to him to come over.

"Congratulations on raising two great rugby boys," said Dan when they were all standing together. He shook hands with Mum, and then Mike. "Even if they have been having a bit of a rough time, lately."

"We're okay, now," said Dylan.

"Dan's been giving us a few tips on how to impress the senior coaches, eh, Dylan?" said Carter.

"They have been through a tough time," said Mum. "Rugby can feel very competitive once the junior years are over."

"Well, as I explained to Dylan and Carter," said Dan, "there's only one way to get to the top in rugby, and that's through teamwork. Everyone has to pull together."

Mike looked uncomfortable.

"I'll catch you all later," said Dan with a smile, turning away. "There are some people from the news waiting to talk to me."

When Dan had gone, Mike looked at Mum.

"I guess parents have to work as a team, too," he said. "I think I could do better on that score."

"Me, too," said Mum. "I think we can be a better example to our boys."

From across the room, Mr Mahaka came striding towards them.

"Well done out there, lads!" he said to Carter and Dylan, slapping them on the back. "When did you boys figure out that great act you put on tonight?"

"Actually, it wasn't too long before we went on the field," said Dylan.

"It was a last-minute plan," added Carter.

"Never seen anything like it!" said Mr Mahaka. "The crowd loved it! I'm looking forward to seeing you both play in the Under 14s A-Grade team next year."

"*If* we get into the A-Grade," said Carter.

Mr Mahaka smiled, as if he had some inside information. "I don't think there's any doubt about that," he said. "Now, enjoy your evening, everyone, and don't be afraid to say hi to the Green Ferns. I'm told they like to meet the locals!"

As Mum prepared to drive out of the club car park that evening, Carter couldn't stop grinning. He'd brought his Dan t-shirt with him, and now the back of it was covered in Green Ferns signatures. Dan had signed his name right across the front!

"What a night!" said Mum.

"It was awesome!" said Carter. "I wish we could do it all over again."

"The best news is that you and Dylan are rugby mates, again," said Mum. "Tell me, how *did* you two come up with your performance?"

Carter looked out the window. Dylan and Mike were getting into their car. Dylan glanced up and waved to Carter, and Carter waved back.

Carter smiled. "We were just trying to be team players, Mum," he said.